How Many Horses

HOW MANY HORSES

DAVID ROMTVEDT

Ion Books
Box 111327
Memphis, TN 38111-1327

Ion Books
P.O. Box 111327
Memphis, TN 38111-1327

A *Raccoon* Book

LIBRARY OF CONGRESS
Library of Congress Cataloging-in-Publication Data

Romtvedt, David.
    How many horses / by David Romtvedt.
        p.   cm.
    ISBN 0-938507-15-X   : $10.95
    I. Title.
    PS3568.05655H69   1988   87-36626
    811'.54--dc19   CIP

Cover photography by David Romtvedt

Book design by David Spicer & Diana Taylor

Acknowledgments

Certain of these poems have previously appeared or will soon appear in magazines. Grateful acknowledgments are due the following:

Casper Star Tribune (1987 Arts Edition): "Dark Image on a Screen" and "Our Distance"

Crab Creek Review: "May I Present" and "Sleeping Under Stars"

Event (Canada): "Before Wyoming" and "Harold's Idea"

High Plains Literary Review: "Thirteen Snapshots"

Nimrod: "Moonrise," "Our Distance," "Our Lady," "Something Inside," and "Summer Circus"

Northern Lights: "Moving Cows" and "Town Life"

Raccoon: "Clever Hans," "For Love," "Glass Canyons," "Posture," "Stone Horses," "Supermarket Horse," and "What I Know"

The Sun (Chapel Hill, NC): "Among People," "Outside Wyoming," "There and Here," and "Wyoming, In Memoriam"

"Fixing Fence" appeared in *Hands, Joining,* an anthology published by Brooding Heron Press, Waldron Island, Washington.

"Four Mile, Ten Below" appeared in the 1988 calendar of the Bainbridge Island Arts Council, Bainbridge Island, Washington. Under the title "February, Ten Below" it was published as an Ion Books/*Raccoon* postcard.

The author thanks the National Endowment for the Arts for an individual fellowship which supported the writing of this book.

I've been influenced by many writers, both those I know personally and those I know only through their words. Thanks to Lee Bassett, B. J. Buckley, Galway Kinnell, Mary Jane Knecht, John Lane, David Lee, Richard Shelton, Floyd Skloot, Wallace Stevens, Shinkichi Takahashi, Emily Warn and William Carlos Williams. I'm grateful also to the people of northern Wyoming — Maggie and John Iberlin, ranchers at Wormwood; Dollie and Simon Iberlin, ranchers at Four Mile; Dr. Tom Berry, veterinarian from Buffalo; Mary Juanicotena and the members of the Bighorn Basque Club; and Marian and Jean Cinquambre.

Final thanks to a border collie named Cleo, and to the horses — Trouble, Penelope, Harold, Coy, Pony and The Bitch.

For Margo

Contents

Four Mile, Ten Below

We walk three hours
toward Powder River
looking for horses.

They see us,
lift their heads
and drift over a hillside,

winter breath
for us to ride.

What I Know

Today Trouble threw me, turning
at full gallop on his own.
Now I brush him, his head hanging
lower as he begins to relax. I whisper
his names — T-Bone, Mr. T, The Walker,
not a troublesome bone in his body.
I move to Ms. P., brush the dried sweat
from her coat. The P is for Penelope
but more often we call her P-Brain
as she stumbles across ditches
and trips on every rock. Brushed,
she too begins to relax. The others,
unridden, get the once-over — Harold,
who Margo says is ugly and who scares
himself when he puts his head
in a bucket of oats. His forehead
bangs the bucket, the oats rattle
and he jerks out before he can eat.
Coy, who I call Coy-Boy, golden coat
and trimmed mane, who lunges
at Harold every chance he gets,
ears back, lips curled. The pony,
who has no name but Pony,
and who no one rides, matted dense coat,
hind hooves long curl forward
from being foundered, his slow
saunter behind the big horses. Last,
there's the old black horse, the lady
everyone calls The Bitch. She's not
so bad, I claim, though her ears
are always back. One last stroke
along her rump then I turn and, tired,
lean on her to watch the vast

banks of clouds skim across
the watery blue sky while she eats.
As my eyes close, she quickly lifts
her head, turns, and bites my forearm —
not bad, just to let me know.

Where The Deer Have Slept

I love stumbling upon the places
where the deer have slept
the night before, the room-sized
circle of flattened grass.
And when I get off, the horse
noses there but does not eat.
I lie down on my back.
My eyes close and I tuck
my arms tightly to my sides
then roll until within that circle
I come to the edge.

Our Distance

Dear Belem,

Great time and far places
since we were one. Remember? I am happy
now in this great empty land made of dust.
Even without water and under the incessant
blue sky into which everyone squints.

I am riding horses, great monstrous friends
who I would swear, Belem, know the most
sealed places of our damaged hearts.

At first I feared the horses,
could not, as any child here comfortably can,
hold a handful of corn under a horse's mouth.
Now fear is gone — I rub their black nostrils,
press my cheek to theirs, lift their feet
to remove a stone, comb out their tails.

One horse — Trouble — I especially care for.
As I brush him, he begins to relax.
His head drops and his eyes half close.
Fully at ease, his penis falls out
of its foreskin in a great pink arc.

This is true life here, Belem. It's funny —
all I tell you must seem trivial,
but it is trivial the way water is,
flowing in a stream, and the stream
is always leaving home and coming home.

Late Winter Circus

From our second floor bedroom window
the electric line sways across the yard
to the wooden pole near the barn.

To impress you I don spangles and tights,
step along the wire and at the pole leap
down onto dirty snow. Barefoot on ice

I throw the barn door open. The music
it makes banging the wall is more beautiful
than the greatest symphony. I whistle

and Trouble trots out, braided tail and mane,
bells around his neck, sequined bridle.
I leap up onto his back and in the cold late

winter night we ride in circles illumined
by the yard light while you applaud
from the window and blow kisses

that melt like spring snow on warming ground.
Now, confidently, Trouble speeds up
as, on his back, I stand on my hands.

Moonrise

We step out on the porch
to watch the sky blackening
from blue. Out across
the pasture the shapes
of two horses slowly move.
The moon rising before them,
they seem to step
purposefully toward it.

Having walked daily
in their field I know
they approach a particular
cottonwood where there is hay
and a chipped porcelain bathtub
filled with water. When they drink
it is long, Penelope especially,
long noisy drafts of light
reflected in water. Two horses
in darkness swallow the moon.

Moving Cows

Why the ranch is called Four Mile I don't know — forty miles from town. And the Bridge Pasture — two thousand acres without a bridge. Never know for naming things, but that's where we're going. Some of Harriets' cows — six or maybe nine — got in somewhere and we're gonna take those cows back out.

We've got to go load the saddles onto the old Jeep flatbed with the trailer hitch, make sure there's gas, drive south of town to Gladys Esponda's to get the horse trailer, then up to Simon's pasture that's trapped between two Interstates to get the horses — take Trouble, Ms. P., and Harold. Probably only need two but never can tell.

Trouble's ok, he walks right up and in. Ms. P., she's a little harder — got to be coaxed. Gets her front legs up but can't seem to see how she's gonna get those hind ones over the sill, cracks her shin and leaps forward, ok. Now Harold's the hard one, got to prop the door so it can't swing in the wind, the rusty noise makes him skitter. Got to beg and cajole and tug and push all at once, pick up a foot and set it in the trailer, then pick up another, push him forward and pick up a hind foot. For five minutes he stands there like that three feet in and one kind of hanging in midair. Me and Margo can't believe it. We just stand there waiting to see what he'll do — nothing. Finally, I lift that last foot and, with the flat of my hand, hit the metal wall of the trailer. When it clangs, Harold's in.

Now we drive down the gravel road to the Interstate and out of town toward Powder River twenty miles, get off at Schoonover Road and rattle along twenty more, six eagles on fenceposts, sheep every which where you look, deer and pronghorn, way out here just dust and deep eroded washes, sage and greasewood. You think it's gonna be real quiet when you turn off the engine but no, oil rigs everywhere, oil companies always looking for more, and always looking where Simon doesn't own the mineral rights.

So finally we find those cows all scattered out along the creek standing in the shade of the cottonwoods, not bunched up like cows ought to be. We unload the horses, saddle them and start scooting around moving cows this way and that. Simon goes ahead opening gates we go through, and closing them. Every once in a while some cow takes off back where we came from and Margo goes to turn it our way, or I go —no ropes cause we don't know how to use them.

Finally, Harriets' cows are all where they belong and I lift Harold's feet back up in the trailer so we can do the whole forty miles in reverse and put the horses back and the trailer, the Jeep, the saddles, when Hell, we could have moved those cows just walking around talking to them.

Something Inside

Dear Belem,

Daily we have to wash the bitter taste
from our mouths, and no matter
the soap that taste comes back.
For several letters I haven't been able
to tell you this story — our mare Marthe,
the four-year-old, kept going into Cyprien's pasture.
I think she was in love with his old bay Tom.
Cyprien would lead Marthe back and all leather
voiced say, "You keep that mare outa my field.
You don't, I'm gonna do something." I didn't
know. What would Cyprien do? He threatens
everyone. And Marthe wanted to go over there.

One day Cyprien comes walking up leading Marthe.
Her eyelids are shut kind of crumpled
and there's blood on her face. Cyprien
walks straight up to the house and he throws
two eyeballs down in front of me — Marthe's eyes.

You can't believe, Belem, how big
a horse's eyes are. Cyprien shows me
his knife and how he took the pointed end
of the blade, slipped it gently in the corner
of both sockets and popped her eyes out.
Like that. And he walks away. "She never
gonna find her way into my field again,"
Cyprien says over his shoulder.

How can there be such a wicked balance,
Belem? I could not make out which way
to turn, Marthe just standing there,

her big bones beautiful as ever, quiet
and still. I bent over and threw up,
couldn't shoot her, went to the vet
and he killed her with an injection.

Maybe a cat or a dog you can put to sleep
when it's old but a horse does not go to sleep,
a horse dies. And I tell you, Belem,
I think I might kill Cyprien myself
and not care if it's clean or right.
The nights are dark enough
to make us all blind and the stars
are bullet holes on the windshield
of my old truck.

Dark Image On A Screen

After a February storm
we found the horses, thin as new moons
and nervous as birds. We brought them
back to the cabin, spread hay and cake,
made a fire and slept. Awakened
in the night by the heavy crunch
of hooves on snow, the horses
circling our rooms, the deep blue
silhouettes passing the windows,
the great puffs of breath
in the moonlight, we went out
naked but for boots and walked
the circular path with the horses,
the mysterious winding of a cord
around our beds, whatever it was
they knew it hadn't occurred
to us before to seek.

Thirteen Snapshots

1.

Astonished by horses
the string of Winnebagos
slowed to twenty
and each driver gawked.

2.

Newly shod, each step the clang
of steel on stone, Trouble turns,
apparently amázed by the space behind him.

3.

Along the fence Penelope careens,
hops to the side, half bucks,
a whinny to the wind
for whom she regularly
puts on this show.

4.

Dr. Tom denies emotion
in horses — "Well, maybe
boredom," he grants, "the way
they stand chewing on a fence."

5.

Penelope is beautiful
but her gait is short
so she is slow.
Trouble is beautiful
and can stretch out,
long stride, faster and faster.
Harold is ugly
and only runs when compelled.
His beauty you think about
eyes closed.

6.

The wind blew and snow fell.
For a month, night and day,

the temperature not above zero,
each day shorter and darker.
The thermostat in my house
set at sixty, I sat, wearing
a sweater and drinking tea,
the horses constantly in my mind,
crossing space behind my eyes,
cold as I knew it would grow colder.

7.

The ranchers, grown stringy and tough,
imagine their wives well fed and fat,
driving great pastel Cadillacs to pastures
filled with thoroughbreds and deep green grass,
imagine they will not care
when one horse leans against the mirror
and snaps it off, when a second horse
takes the aerial in his teeth
and bends it ninety degrees.

8.

I speak English, Spanish and French.
I can render greeting
in German, Chinese and Basque.
But only now,
years gone by,
have I begun to speak Horse.

9.

Cresting the hill, five horses.
I could see them —
out of sight, still.

10.

Brushing Harold,
picking out fly eggs
and scraping off dried mud,
I run my hands along his legs,

massage the bulbous joints —
his delicate bony legs.
When I think of him on the run,
I am amazed
and my sudden emotion
makes him jump.

11.

For the August parade
he rode down Main Street
on a sorrel mare,
finely tooled saddle and inlaid spurs,
satin bows in the mare's tail and mane.
Turning to wave, he smiled,
mistaking the bows
for butterflies come to rest.

12.

The wind blows clouds across the sky.
Soon the horses will be running.

13.

By midmorning the air
shimmered in heat,
the flies insanely buzzed.
It was hot
and it would only get hotter.
The horses leaned
in the shadow of a cottonwood.

Traveling

An old woman, blind in her left eye,
her right arm amputated at the elbow,
regular rides Saturday night to Porky's
in UCross. "I left my horse tied
to the unleaded pump," she tells Buzzy
and he, smiling, asks her to tie the horse
up at the rail next to the bar. "You know
that horse gonna get hit by some drunk
in a pick-up you always leave him
out by the pump." And somebody drinking
says, "Or some Jacob gonna steal him."
The Jacob's are honest but they come in
for this kind of noise as they've got
the only other business in UCross —
a junkyard — and their trees are full of turkeys.
The woman waves Buzzy away and to me says,
"I been ranchin' near Clearmont all my life.
Stupid life. What d'ya think? Got at least
two thousand deer on my place but no heart
to kill 'em, so they eat my feed. When the Lord
made Wyoming, he stood up and shaded his eyes
to look out across all those ridges. Somethin'
was wrong — 'looks good, but whoo-ee, it smells
bad.' I love Wyoming — animals and birds
of every kind, big spaces and hardly enough people
for a respectable fistfight." Grinning
and focusing that one good eye on me,
she asked Buzzy for a Bud Light
and stepped outside to move her horse.

For Love

The bones of dead horses
rise from the hills and dress themselves
as grasshoppers or snakes.
That's why horses so skittery
about their feet — don't want to step
on their dead brothers and sisters.

A horse never asks what good
it is doing something — it's all useless,
gonna do the same thing tomorrow and the day after.
Doesn't make a horse unhappy.
Taking it easy. Let the dust do the walking.

Dust wants to be up roiling around,
splaying itself out down the road,
trying to leave the wind behind
and tear the cover off the baby mice
hidden in the hay, smother the leafless trees
bent over. Dust sees everything
while making it all blind.

Horse doesn't mind — turns around
butt into the wind, hangs its head
and pays no attention to the sun's
passage, the illuminated broken everything
in the pasture, all rising up
to cry out for love.

Speech

Dear Belem,

Last night I dreamt I spoke to you,
a thousand miles away, by phone. Even dreaming
I was not courageous enough to let us stand together
in the same room, watching our lips move.

My voice caught in my throat.
"A bad connection," you said, your kindness,
and we hung up.

I tried to dream the telephone was never invented.
We stood on opposite shores of an inland sea
and shouted, our voices rolling with the waves.

Still, I could not speak my mind,
could not say why, years before,
I had turned and told you I would go.

This Wyoming, I thought, high and harsh.
What wild horse drove me far out on a ridge
and keeps me there, where I will never be at home?

Stretching His Head

Through the door
of the van
Coy tears open
the bag of oats

I'd planned
to feed
Penelope, Harold,
The Bitch, Trouble and him.

Think he feels sorry?
Not a chance.
Mouthful of grain,
he closes his mouth and chews.

You Know Whose Horse This Is

Simone called her Cricket,
but Dollie, thinking her more a flower
than a charming large bug,
said she would be Sweet Pea.
Amazed by her stumbling,
Margo claimed she was a P-Brain
but allowed as how most days
she was simply Ms. P., capable
and strong. To me she was
ethereal and shimmering
like some dream willow
in a draw and I said,
"Willow," when she came into sight.
"Willow?" Margo said, "It's too
green. How 'bout Penelope?
Another good name for a beauty
queen." And easily dropped back
to P-Brain. Annoyed
by everyone's frivolous
treatment of his high-class
horse, Simon has taken to calling her
Lady Di. "Djoo check on
Lady Di?" he asks us. "Who?"
we say. "Lady Di," he repeats
very clearly. "Oh, yeah,"
we answer, "P-Brain's fine."
Yes, Ms. P., Penelope, Willow,
Cricket, and Sweet Pea, she's
in the South Pasture,
still able to outrun her name.

Juggling

Margo picks up a brush, bit and halter.
Suddenly they become horseshoes
she throws easily into the air,
coming down as the rodeo arena
in Buffalo, Wyoming.

Up on the hill behind the cabin
I lie among grasshoppers, warm,
clatter and crash, to watch Margo
juggle cottonwood leaves.

I've got a mason jar of water
from which I drink. In one swallow
an entire prairie dog town,
curious about the show.

Still juggling, Margo becomes a horse
carrying a hackamore in her teeth.
I jump up and, bareback, ride,
the dry hot wind riffling my hair
as it lifts my horse's mane
and sends her tail streaming behind.

Seated again on the ground
I notice how hard it is,
how dry and sparse the grass,
how it pokes my skin,
how the dust covers me
and I can't get comfortable,
thinking how sad it is to grow old!

Until Margo pulls my hands and feet
right off my body and juggles all four

amidst the still suspended cottonwood leaves,
inside and outside, over and under,
the juggler's fine art.

She smiles, putting her well-trained
fingers in her pockets. Look,
left on their own, miraculously,
my appendages do not fall.
They become birds,
flap their wings,
and fly.

Town Life

Our veterinarian Tom tells me how strange it feels to have money mixed up with what he loves. Our neighbor Jean Pierre's wife works a job, leaving her husband to care for the house. Because of this, Jean Pierre says he is free. His friend, Pete, who is a retired herder, says this is baloney, that he is more free alone in a sheep wagon up in the Bighorns. "Besides," Pete says, "*free* is a word and words just trap you."

Tom, Jean Pierre and Pete are all right. I want to take a risk and say I believe town life makes the idea of freedom even more confusing. A lot of town people will tell you two things about freedom — some things just naturally have it, and money can buy it.

My aunt came to visit from Omaha. We drove out toward UCross. It was late fall, only a little snow on the ground — cold — and the wind blowing. We saw five horses on a hill, their hair up all electric, breath steaming out of their nostrils, their tails flipping wildly, that insane look in their eyes. My aunt said she envied them their freedom. It's like adults say of children —"Free as a bird." And none of them is free — birds, kids or horses.

Still, the idea persists so that around every town you see horses in half-acre fields. I know it seems bad faith, but I say people with money buy horses they don't need, hoping freedom rubs off when the truth is that a horse like that's only an idea. The good comes when the owner looks closely and the horse once again becomes a horse.

Jean Pierre looks at me like I'm a little off, and Tom says I don't explain it well. Every horse has its horsey problems. The people who've always spent the most time with horses have been the people with the least money. When the oil boom came, people who'd always been poor suddenly had money to spend. They bought new pick-ups, took trips to the Basque Country, stayed in hotels in Denver and Bayonne, bought houses in town. Normal, but things were out of whack.

Everyone knew and stuck by each other. May have been town life, but this town — Buffalo, Wyoming — is small enough that every hook you get yourself caught on thinking it's some bright appealing insect, some neighbor's gonna take you off. A person can leave a ranch behind but the land stays there, not exactly waiting for anything, but waiting.

So far it's true that after the boom comes the bust. No one is born a God, but all can grow to be. When there's more money to be made speculating on real estate than working the land, then every person has to decide which matters.

Oh, I don't know, I started out trying to talk about freedom and money and living in town. I was pretty confident. But honestly, I don't think I've got the mind for it. I kind of swing around at a subject instead of homing in on it. I was just thinking that way out here in Wyoming the news of the world heads our way and though we come as unglued as anyone, we try to keep to ourselves and hang onto our horses even when there's not much left for them to do.

Sleeping Under Stars

Dear Belem,

Still dark I wake,
some dream horse galloping
across my chest.
I reach out to hold it
and fold my arms
around the deep black sky.

But the sky is a polished mirror
into which, even with eyes closed,
I see. I am holding myself
and the cold stars
burn my skin.

Oh, my absent one,
the one who is me,
when do I come home?
When does the first red flower
break into bloom?

Torture

A human being is hurt for long periods
in a small sealed room far away from me —
the scar where a knife entered flesh,
the meter measuring pain I've come to see.

I look at the horse I've been riding
and cling to it, push my face
into its sweating neck, the warm smooth hair,
the rank agreeable odor of horse,

of which nothing human, however
I may use it, is even slightly like.

Old Horse

This year John Iberlin's old horse
didn't come in with the others
when I dumped hay from the truck.

We crosscut the ridgelines
looking up and down the draws,
walked twice to the river and back.

Once at dusk facing the sun,
I saw the horses crest a hill,
black shapes before the light.

I couldn't tell who was who,
just horses in a bunch on the run.
Were there seven, or only six?

In Spring, I walked again, lurching
through mud and worn out snow.

And I looked at bones, checking
for cow or deer or horse.

A Wyoming Myth

In January of 1966 an old Crow woman, tired of her age and the palsied chattering of her body, walked from Powder River up Crazy Woman Creek into the Bighorns. She thought she would be as the original Crazy Woman, an Indian dying alone in the snow. But when she reached the spot where Crazy Woman had died, the old woman slipped out of her skin and dropped it to the ground.

Young again, the old woman turned to walk away and stumbled. Confused, she only then realized there was a smell in the air, the smell of horse, and the smell was she. Inhaling deeply, she could smell both herself and her fallen skin — the old Crow woman ready to die and the beautiful young roan mare.

She galloped back to Powder River where her granddaughter was sitting in their cabin staring at a portable radio and listening to President Johnson announce the resumption of bombing of North Vietnam. The old-woman-young-horse whinnied and banged on the door with her hoof. The granddaughter opened the door and, seeing only a horse in the yard, closed the door again. Then opened it. Strange horse, not theirs, not one of the white rancher's. The horse ran in circles, its tail arched high, great clouds of breath steaming from its nostrils.

The horse stopped and stared at the granddaughter, who didn't know what to say. And it was cold so she closed the door and sat down again in front of the radio. Again the old-woman-young-horse banged at the door. Opening it, the granddaughter shooed the horse, now making a nuisance of itself, away. She didn't recognize her grandmother's eyes in the face of the horse.

A third time the horse banged at the door, battering it with both hooves. Annoyed, the granddaughter filled a bucket of water, opened the door and flung the water on the horse. Immediately coated with ice, the horse turned and galloped back up Crazy Woman Creek. As carefully as possible, she picked up her old woman skin in her teeth and draped it across her frozen back, where it slowly melted the ice and slid into place — the stooped shoulders, liver-spotted hands, frostbitten ears and nose.

The old woman limped home, a little frozen blood where her horse's teeth had bitten through the skin of her ankle. She opened the door, walked in and sat down next to her granddaughter. Only then, sliding her feet on the floor, did she notice the blood and bend down to see what was wrong. And only then did the granddaughter turn off the radio and ask her what had happened.

Limp

Almost dusk, we ride, Dr. Tom and I,
crossing boundaries into countries of cold
and night. Distant, through the glass,
a lone wild horse. "Look," Tom says,
"at his right shoulder, muscle torn loose,
stallion fight in a herd I'll bet.
Watch the way he limps when he walks."

Staring, I can see the rotten flesh,
oozing pus. Tom uses the doctor term —
weeping lesion. "A horse hurt like that
the others drive away, always. It's the smell."
And we ride home across rocky earth,
clatter of shod hooves ringing in our ears.

Firecracker

Dear Belem,

They say the dead remain
inside us when they are gone. Maybe
that's true but still they are gone.
Forgive me my continuing insistence
on writing of the horses as if they
were people or as important as people.
Perhaps it is self-indulgent in these days
of nuclear bombs and people's present pain
in South Africa, in Salvador, in the Middle East,
in our own rich countries, Belem,
and I won't try to deceive you
with talk of animals as metaphors
for universal human values.
The simple truth is I have come to care
for the horses and maybe I do believe
they are as important as we are.

Strangely, Belem, sharing our lives with us,
they come to share our ailments and deaths.
Did you know horses get cancer?
It is not even rare. The most common
is malignant melanoma — in all horses,
though mostly grays. Appaloosas and white horses
suffer squamous cell carcinoma, a skin cancer.
All these words — soon there will be horse oncologists.
Even to me that feels somehow frivolous,
oncologists with their words — *sonogram,*
nuclear scanner, gamma scanner, hard radiation machine,
lymphoma and lymphocyte — and their diagnoses —
equal parts biochemistry, voodoo and intuition.

See how I'm wound up on this subject.
You know, Belem, the story I'm leading toward,
the way I lead a horse toward a trailer

inside which he'll ride to the vet's.
It was eighty-year-old Jean Irigaray's racer
Firecracker, who was twenty-six himself
and hadn't been on a track in years.
Firecracker's cancer was the melanoma.
Jean knew nothing of what went on inside
his horse's body. Dr. Tom explained that
most likely the bad cells filled Firecracker,
that they had entered the lymphatic system,
maybe the kidney and liver. Little could be done
though Tom explained he could destroy lumps
along the skin — cut them out, or burn them,
or freeze them with nitrogen. Jean was heartbroken,
Belem, a true breaking of his heart.
Horse or human, Jean didn't think.
He asked could nothing else be done?
Dr. Tom said he would call the CSU vet school
and get back to us in a few days.

I drove Jean home and, though it was cold,
we walked in the pasture. The wind was wailing
so the dried leaves spun and danced
like a brain storm. "Twenty-six years,"
Jean said, and I think he meant everything —
the pasture, the irrigation ditch and dams,
the battered fenceposts and worn barbed wire,
the way the clouds boil so thick layers
shift and fly, opening and closing
windows onto the blue. This
is not sentimental bullshit, Belem.
For some, these horses are their only
union with another world.

On Wednesday I drove Jean back to the vet's.
Dr. Tom felt all over Firecracker's body.
He ran both hands together along the horse's neck,

hard questioning fingers, warm.
He told Jean there were small bumps everywhere,
cancer all through the body. I kept quiet, Belem,
seeing Firecracker's insides as a garden
of foul flowers all blossoming at once —
inky bloody blooms, poisonous pollen, barbs and ash.

At the base of the neck Tom used an electric knife
to cut out a lump — sizzle of hair and flesh —
and, though the horse was anaesthetized,
he could smell it and in terror bashed against
the padded walls of the squeeze chute. Exposed,
the lump was a dull rubbery blob, somnolent
and benign. Quick-frozen, sliced and dyed,
it was analyzed. Later there were core samples
of bone marrow — hollow needles drilled into
Firecracker's pelvis, then blood and urine analysis.
Into the loose soft skin between his front legs
dyes were injected. All this went on
at the university down in Colorado.
"Just like a human," they told Jean,
"we can do radiation, chemotherapy, treatment
just like a human . . ."

But you can talk to a human, Belem,
and nowadays, on humans even, the plug
is pulled and people go home to die
in their living rooms, the busy world
at the window, friends and family passing
in and out. And wouldn't a horse rather
stand in the shade of a cottonwood
or lean against the south wall of a shed
in a winter wind than die in a building
smelling of antiseptic and soap and human?

We just don't let go, do we?
As part of an experiment, CSU paid

for most of it, still Jean spent $3000.
He told me money doesn't matter.
For a horse, Belem. I shut up
knowing he'd been for fifty years
one of the stingiest of the carefully stingy
Basque ranchers. He even went down there
and stayed in a motel — a characterless room
with a copy of a western landscape
above the bed, a plastic drinking cup
sealed in a plastic bag by the sink,
a TV with cable and HBO.

I pictured Jean rising alone each day,
dressing carefully for a good day.
I wanted to go down with him
but didn't ask, thinking I was ghoulish.
I remembered Jean's wife, dead three years,
and wondered if this attention was connected,
another way Jean mourned that loss.
It was a cheap thought, for what mattered
to Jean, as strongly as his wife had mattered,
was the horse, the integrity of its life.

It's another thing these people, these animals,
this place has taught me. I don't have to
tell you what, you know. And, Belem,
I promise you, I'll never forget.

Late At Night

After long days riding,
moving sheep from Four Mile
to the mountains, Margo's
grandfather comes home,
enters his darkened house.
Negotiating the turns
from memory, he finds
a box of matches,
strikes one. The blue tip
flames, illuminating
the room, thickly
shadowed, an old man's
face. He seems to wait
then looks up, grins,
"Of course," as if
remembering an important
event far away. "Of
course," he repeats,
pulling the string
that hangs in front
of him. "Electricity,
I forget about
electricity."

And Wyoming Has The Lowest
Population Of All The States

Hot day. No horses.
Hiked the Bighorns
to Seven Brothers Lakes,
rocky and clear, snowfed
water, the slopes
littered with boulders
and, even in June,
patches of snow.
The Seven Brothers
have no names, are marked
only by wooden plaques —
Lake number one or three
or seven, say.
At the far western end,
wrapped around the last lake's
cobbled shore, a cliff,
striated and bare, rising
to 10,000 feet, then more.
Made camp there.
Took off my clothes
and crawled into cold water,
whooping and splashing.
Came out and put on a shirt
but no pants, large body
grown from small penis,
shivering like aspen leaf
on its stem. Made a fire
and sat in the smoke
away from bugs — gnats
and mosquitos and flies —
thinking this place
is thick with bugs,
but then, Jesus no,
this world is thick
with us.

Stone Horses

In Athens, buried in the northeast corner
of the Parthenon is a stone horse,
thousands of years old and thousands of miles
from our horses grazing at the base
of the Bighorns. Every year that old Greek
building shifts slightly and the stone horse
is buried a little deeper in rubble,
just as every year our horses go a little deeper
into winter, and come out in spring distant,
the haunted look in their eyes colder,
their bodies increasingly gaunt.

"Oh, If You Could Know"

Down there, that's where we rode
through the greasewood, in the field.
About a mile that way, I called those
the Lizard Rocks cause I'd go there
and hunt lizards, all day, loved lizards,
and snakes, and horned toads who pushed
against my hand when I'd pet them.
I thought they liked it
so I'd turn them over and stroke
their bellies. They seemed hypnotized.
Later I learned that upside down
horned toads passed out.

I kept chameleons in the houseplants
and turtles in the bathtub. In winter
I'd get so excited when I found a fly.
You know how flies freeze
then if it gets warm they wake up
but they're woozy and easy to catch.
I'd grab them and feed them to my lizards.

I climbed over every rock
poking a stick into each crack and hole,
wiggling the stick in the sand
looking for Swifts hiding from the heat.
But you had to be careful
cause there might be a rattlesnake
and scorpions sleep in the sand, too.
I never took water or food —
too busy for that — but when I got back,
covered with dust, I was starving,
dying of thirst, and late.

This dry ranch and these horses
are my state of grace.
I don't forget any of it, even what I hate,
like when Simon made me help kill prairie dogs.
I caught a baby one and wanted to save it,
but Simon made me put it back in the hole
and pour in the poison oats. I cried
and he never made me do it again.

We used to trail sheep from Four Mile
to Wormwood because there weren't any scales
at Four Mile then. All day we'd ride
following the sheep. At night
we'd sleep on the ground
next to the animals and the stars.

I was afraid I'd screw up
but I loved it anyway. I'd try to keep the sheep
together. Simon would say to other ranchers,
"This is Margo; she's my top hand."
And look proud. But alone, he'd yell at me
for my mistakes, and once I did lose
an entire band of sheep Simon had to find.

Then there was docking —
we'd get up at 3:00 a.m. day after day
and cut tails and testicles off lambs
until everyone and even the earth
was blood-soaked and sticky
and we were standing in blood-mud.

Long summer days, my cousin Brad and I
would ride to Powder River, seven miles
from the cabin at the end of the ranch.
We'd pick up fallen branches and pretend

to be knights in armor, aim our cottonwood lances
at each other's hearts, galloping
as fast as we could, at the last minute
veering away so we never hit each other.
We'd just run and run and run.

That's it — I've been happiest with horses.
I can't tell you how it feels inside
or what horses mean or why childhood
in this dry empty spot, more barren
and desolate, you know that's what people
think about Wyoming, especially here,
this dry ugly desert of cactus and cold,
no trees, a little yellow grass.
But I look around and everything's
alive — the greasewood field, the Lizard Rocks,
Brad and me with our cottonwood lances,
the horses and the long ride to the river
and for all of it, I never wanted to go home,
just wanted to be there, be here. Come on,
today we'll ride, you and me, and you'll see.

Summer Circus

Long days, the sun going down slow
and distant, a swelling of purple, red and rose
over the Bighorns, real clouds with silver
linings, and the cottonwoods' shimmering leaves.

No costume could compete so one warm evening
dressed in nothing I appear fully decked out
for the circus of the naked animals,
the only show of its kind in Wyoming.

I throw my hands into the sky and as ringmaster
announce the main event — "Ladies (to Margo
on the porch) and Gentlemen (to the grasses
and trees). Tonight, for one night only,

the most unbelievable . . ." But before I can finish
Trouble bangs the barn door open (right on cue)
and lopes into the yard, untouched by blanket
or bridle, not even a fly in his mane.

He trots in a tight circle, gloriously naked,
his body glittering in the reflected light.
Cleo, our arthritic old Border Collie, appears
collarless. She does her best to gambol,

and, truly, she's as happy as we to be without
her clothes, standing on her hind legs
and turning round and round, barking at Trouble
with each revolution, panting in between.

"Yes, ladies and gentlemen, these gallant performers
know best, no need for lengthy introductions

or boring speeches, it's on with the show."
So as Trouble tightens his circle and Cleo

keeps trying to turn, I climb the windmill
and leap into the stock tank. Surfacing I smile
and call out, inviting the audience forward
to join the show and it works — here's Margo,
unbuttoning her shirt and unlacing her shoes.

History

Dear Belem,

Wormwood and Four Mile — two big ranches,
thousands of acres and Harriets' place even bigger,
in winter all slate gray and bone empty, steely
low sky, only a few people roaming over the emptiness,
dragging a living out of it, pushing sheep and cows.

I remember the ghosts, Belem, the old ones
who came before us, who never stood in the glare
of a halogen yard lamp, never rode across a field,
electricity whirring in wires overhead.

Luke, a Wind River Shoshone, appeared drunk,
knocked on my door, didn't speak, left.
Next morning, he crawled out from under the porch.

All the smashed pick-ups — the Fords upside down
in ditches, slid off the sides of frozen mountains,
mashed head-on into walls, fences, somebody's new house
or barn, other pick-ups. Smashed, they come to a stop
and, inside, one more dial on a blinded bloody heart
refuses to turn. I am ashamed, Belem,

of what we've made of the land and of those
once who lived with it. From the Interstate
you see miles of grassland, mountains, trees
high on the slopes. In spring the creeks
come ripping down new courses. From a distance
the surface looks fine but you can't see shit
from the window of a car driving the Interstate.

This was our only home, this
arid heaving body that is nearly dead.
Oh, hell, Belem, if Wyoming were a K-Mart,
the damned state would be a blue-light special
on disaster.

The fights — Fort Fetterman, Fort Phil Kearny
the Wagon Box, the Little Bighorn. Even the mosses
and lichens quiver in fear of us. The screams of the dead
refuse to fade as they rise to Heaven, and the sins
of the fathers are visited upon the sons.

Look, Belem, I'm a white American alive
in the last years of the twentieth century.
It took my people two generations to unravel
another people's way of life, to unravel biology.
Not even Wyoming stays the same — Cheyenne,
Shoshone, Sioux, Blackfoot, Crow, gone,
artifacts stolen, seeds scattered. I can't
get too close to this, I'm no Indian.

Just say I'm wrong — the people are alive
and will come back. Leave all this behind
and wander, eyes caressing the hills.
Ignore the fences and signs, the nomads in airplanes,
the buffalo buried in a park, and the bear,
who when they roam are shot or drugged, tagged
and flown up on the last narrow ridge,
the backbone of the world, broken back.
There are no wolves and the mountain lions retreat
higher and higher. The coyote find their way
so we've hired a bounty hunter who killed
4000 last year. I lie down in dream and try
to greet my animal brother. I'm sorry, Belem,

I rant and preach and condemn, but it's because
I feel stupid and weak. Even the life under the earth,
the roots, we know how to kill — drilling rigs,
open pit mines, pipelines. Geology can teach us
to peel back any part of the planet's face, strip it
to the bone. I leave out my part, my car and truck,
my natural gas heated house and steel fence,
the grapefruit I eat shipped from Texas to my table.

I'm part of it, Belem. I know that but don't know
what to do. It's like being so drunk that when
the music stops I don't hear the change, or so tired
I drive straight off the roof of the world
and come down, my face and forehead smashing
through the windshield, blood and glass and bone
but I feel no pain. I'm afraid, Belem, afraid
nothing we know will save us, and nothing
we do will change what we've made. There,
a message that, for once,
I'm happy to know you'll never read.

Comanche

Found bleeding profusely from six wounds,
it would have been a kindness to have cut his throat,
but the soldier could not.

Found in a clump of trees, collapsed,
the order was given to shoot him,
but another soldier didn't have the heart.

Found sitting on his haunches
braced back on his forefeet
pocked with bullets and arrows.

Found standing, his saddle
turned under his belly,
the blanket and pad missing.

Found at the Indian village
with seven grievous wounds, "each of which
would have killed an ordinary horse . . ."

Found in a ravine,
skewered twenty-eight times.

He was led to the river,
bathed and bandaged,
led twelve more miles and put on a boat
to Fort Lincoln. There he could not walk
and was carried in a sling — Comanche,
a 925 pound fifteen-hand-tall bay horse
with twelve official battlefield scars,

the single survivor of the Little Bighorn,
Comanche, unable to walk,
not even the ghosts would ride away.

More Injuries

And young horses are curious, too,
Dr. Tom says. They'll try
to stick their heads into anything,
want to bite and twist at stuff.
When they realize they're caught,
they panic and try to pull out,
no matter what.

All kinds of facial fractures —
they get funny bumps
around their eyes, a crooked
nose, scars along their jaws.
Ever after they're afraid
of small openings, won't
put their heads in a bucket.

Some, though, don't seem to learn.
They go on pushing into spots
they can't get out of,
panic, pull, and more fractures —
funnier looking by the year
and more curious, too.

Two Guys

Riding Harold, a twelve year old Bay quarterhorse,
I stop and get down to pee. Gently, for Harold,
a nervous mister, still fears the smell of people
and the sounds they make as they move.
Even the delicacy of urine falling on earth
might make him spook and want to whirl.

But today, instead of backing up,
Harold twists his head and nudges it
into my shoulder. Surprised, I look to see
his hind legs spread and pink penis hanging,
horse piss and human as noisy as a waterfall
muffling the sounds of the wind in the trees.

Favorite Song

George claims every horse's favorite song
is "Streets of Laredo"
and sings it for Penelope —
        da-daa-da-da, da-da,
        da-daa-da-da, da-da.
"See," he says as she turns her head
his way, "Proof."

But last winter at Four Mile
walking toward Margo's Lizard Rocks
in full sun, ten below, glittering snow,
we stopped to lean on the south side
of a ledge and Johnny Lane explained
horses prefer "I'm an Old Cowhand From the Rio Grande"
and he made up a new first line —
"I'm an old cowgirl from another world . . .
Wyoming, dontcha know," he laughed,
"Another world," and started a snowball fight
with Margo, "UFO's, alien beings, uninhabitable."

We walked on two more hours
and finally found the horses
all winter jumpy so it took a long time
to settle them down and get a rope on one.
But we did and set off walking home,
the other horses trailing the one we led,
Johnny's shoes making what to winter-shy horses
is a scary sound, frozen leather creaking
like a haywire song in the crusty snow
as, unsure of ditches and drifts,
we walked an unsteady pace. Like that,
Margo, Johnny and me made up the rest
of "I'm an Old Cowgirl From Another World."

When I wave my arms I fly
and I can smell you with my eyes.
On my horse I never ride
though she's always by my side.
Well you may think I'm strange
but I understand the range.

Got a neoprene rope, polyurethane chaps,
stainless steel boots and a fiberglass hat,
wear my mylar gloves on my long hairy arms,
yipee ky yo ky yea, whoo.
Yipee ky yo ky yea.

On Saturn's rings I learned to rope
down a planetary slope.
Caught a comet by the tail,
through the universe I sail.
Got no federal graze permit,
ain't got no federal government.
Escaped the bureaucratic mess,
so no galactic neural stress.

Got a neoprene rope, polyurethane chaps,
stainless steel boots and a fiberglass hat,
wear my mylar gloves on my long hairy arms,
yipee ky yo ky yea, whoo.
Yipee ky yo ky yea.

In March we're roping cows on Mars,
by June we're flying to the stars.
Working seven days a week,
and I ain't never seen a sheep.
Antelope and floating deer

browsing on the atmosphere.
Yes, I'm an old cowgirl
from another world.

I'm an old cowgirl from another world
over and over, singing till we'd memorized
what we'd made, we walked through the snow
thinking how George, if he could see us,
even if he admitted the horses were following
along sweet as you please the rope unhitched,
and even if he believed we'd invented some great
words, and even if we offered him a forever warm
bed on a February cold night, even all this,
George would say "Streets of Laredo" 's
every horse's favorite song.

Posture

Riding Harold, I breathe with his gait,
his breath, attend to the rhythmic being
in the world. As he gallops
I lean forward and lay my cheek
against his neck, drop my arms
and stretch my hands along his legs,
hugging myself to this run.

When Harold walks I lean back,
my spine against his,
my head resting on his hip.
He wanders where he will
while I stare at the sky

until my skull bounces on his rump
and, alarmed, Harold bolts forward.
Spinning from side to side
I sit up and lean forward again,
whisper in his ear, "Harold,
it's alright, it's only me."

The Art Of Riding

First you must find the horse.

Live with it, walk for miles
not thinking of riding, sit in one spot
at the base of a hill watching
the horse eat, feel the sky
and listen to the wind.

In winter stay out there with it,
make sure there's hay and alfalfa cake,
corn and oats, check after blizzards,
sleep out of doors as much as you can.
When it's so cold you think you will lose
your fingers and toes, sleep near a fire.

Sometimes the beauty of all this
will put its fingers around your throat,
choking you. You'll laugh and cry, run
screaming through the burnt-out fields,
the dry washes, the snow-drifted draws.

Sometimes it will all be ugly.
You will throw up,
want to knife your children,
chop down the willow you planted,
poison the well you live by.

Now you will be able to touch
the horse and speak without making it bolt.
Your smell will be ordinary
and the strangeness of your gait
no longer strange. Put your arm
around the horse's neck, lean
on its shoulder as the horse leans back.
Run your hands over the horse's body,
the hard naked skin of your hands
over the soft dense hair of horse.

Massage the horse. Learn every lump
and scar and dent this Wyoming,
this blistering frozen and wind-ravaged
land can give, its only gift.

Take a saddle, the lightest
and plainest you can find,
and show it to the horse.
Set it on the ground and step back.
Wait for as long as you can.
You will never ride the horse
but you and it are going to ride.

Go ahead and put the saddle on the horse,
pull tight the girth, speak out loud
to no one of distance and speed and clouds,
then walk again on your own.
Wherever the saddled horse goes, go.
Day and night, summer and winter,
time ticking the change in the hills,
snowmelt, rock falls, a creek
altering its course.

There is more preparation
but I leave it to you to find
the rest of the way — the halter, the bit
and bridle, the stirrups and reins.
One morning you will sit atop the horse,
your breathing almost able to stop.
One moment.

If this feels exaggerated
or contrived, get down,
remove the saddle and move to town.
There it will occur to you
that you might tell the story
of it all — the entire history
of the horse. You decide.

Two Kisses

Dear Belem,

Our house. Once that would have been
David and Belem's. Don't you think
that would have been possible? Our house.
Filled with objects touched by our hands,
redolent of our love. Love stays real.
It is vulgar to speak of new love
or, if not vulgar, lame, but I believe
you would love Margo as much as I do,
and feel at home in our house. Easy to say
since there is no chance you will come.
As for Margo, she already loves you,
has heard so much of your life,
of that distant foreign land I call
only The Past. Margo knows it. Even here,
where some things are so much simpler
I am ashamed to ever complain, or claim
life is hard. Even here there is the past
that separates us and makes us one.
We have talked of giving our child
your name — Belem. I know it would be strange
in this land of Steves, Mikes, Roberts
and Todds, of Melissas, Marys, Kellys
and Annes. Even the good old Basque names
are dying out. So it would be strange
but it is a good name, Belem,
and they will get used to it.
Once this talk could have hurt you —
Margo and me and a child not yours
bearing your name. Insensitive, cruel.
That's the least of our worries now, eh Belem,
whether we hurt each other's feelings,

or act in the right way, the acceptable way?
I say your name aloud — Belem — and picture
the child, a little wild, climbing cottonwoods,
skating on the lake in winter, taking a horse
and riding up into the mountains to stare
at the sky from slightly closer. Maybe
the horse will be named Mexico. Or let's
name it Salvador. Why not, we called
the kid Belem. And whose savior
will Salvador be? I meant to tell
you about the house, the barn
with its wide double doors, the windmill
and pump, the stock pond, fixing fence
and feeding sheep. Oh well, next time.
There'll always be a next time.
For you, Belem, two kisses
from us all — from the new Belem,
from Margo, from me, two kisses —
one for the past,
and one for now.

There, and Here

In Africa, I lived in a village where some boys
caught a monkey and tied a rope around its neck,
pinched it, slapped it, threw stones at its face.
When the monkey cried, the boys leaned back
and laughed, both sounds as close as my breath.

Paraded up the street in pain and exhaustion,
the imprisoned monkey fainted but its keepers
brought it round to suffer some more.
It tried to bare its teeth, as monkeys will,
but this inspired no fear. They were only teeth,
as beautiful as eucalyptus leaves on the trees
where monkeys live above goats and pigs
and flies buzzing like tiny green jars.

In DuBois, Wyoming a rancher was pissed at his horse.
He tied it to the bumper of his pick-up
and dragged it down the county road,
asphalt a high-speed whip
flaying the horse till it died.

A woman here wanted to punish her horse.
She tied him with a rope to the ceiling
of his stall. If he moved, he'd choke.
She left him there three days.

Today is Tuesday, 50 degrees, a cool wind
from the northeast. Lovely day.
I'd meant to go riding
but this one day I won't.

Shearing

The horses off alone in the Bridge Pasture, we're up by the sheds set up to shear John Iberlin's 1900 sheep from Wormwood. Early spring and still cool, but not so cold as to freeze man or sheep, both naked and skinny and nicked by the blades. Australian migrant crew travels all over the West hauling trailers, portable shearing factories.

We bunch the sheep up, bring them in, separate them into groups of fifty and put them in a series of corrals, all day moving forward till they end up in a long narrow pen funneling to a one sheep wide chute. We ease them along, pushing and pulling. Sometimes a sheep leaps straight up into the air. You gotta grab it fast, pull it back down into the chute. If it gets over the wall, you gotta chase it down and drag it back.

"Jumpers," Johnny says, "have to stop 'em. Once a sheep knows it can jump out, it'll try it every time."

I picture myself a sheep — herded along, dogs barking, men running and shouting and smoking, the noise from the unknown trailer — buzz of motor driven shears, grunts of men, the gas-powered generator, other sheep bleating and stinking. Too much happening. Then it stops — the men stand around eating apples and candy bars, paying no attention. Then it starts again. All you can see coming down the chute's the sheep in front of you and a little hole of darkness you walk through.

The door slams like a guillotine in reverse, a hand reaches out, grabs a sheep and yanks it in. Shearer strips the body in two minutes — two hundred sheep a day, two hundred bleary quasi-souls who by this time have given up trying to understand, given up resisting, a glazed look in their eyes.

We keep at it — moving sheep, separating sheep, bunching up sheep, opening and closing gates for sheep, cutting out Labady's and Miro's stray sheep in with Iberlins'. Finished, the shearer slides the oily fleece one way and shoves the sheep the other, out another tiny door and down a board ramp into an unknown world. Sheep falls to the ground dazed, maybe gives a leap into the air like a pronghorn — arched back — sometimes stumbles like a cow on a rock, often bleeding from the shears.

Some doors sheep almost always come out bloody — cuts around the eyes, ears, anus, deep gouges in the flank. Other doors the sheep are never cut. John notices but says nothing to the Australian boss.

Other side of the trailer women hurry to pick up wool, jam it in huge sacks, put the sacks onto a compacter and tie them off making bales twelve feet long, four feet around, three hundred pounds. We roll each bale down the hill, lift it up onto the flatbed — damned hard — then drive and unload in a shed, the bales stacked upright like cigars.

Shearing goes on — generator whine, machine buzz and animal bleat. Johnny's checking and talking, keeps a fire going, painting brands on shorn sheep. "Buyers say we can't paint 'em anymore," he tells me, "too much trouble cleaning the fleece before it's dyed. Sheep'll have big fluorescent ear tags." Johnny keeps painting. "And no more black wool either."

Too bad since black sheep have always been kept in a certain proportion to the total number of sheep — one black per hundred, say. That way a herder just counts the number of black sheep to know how many sheep there are in a band.

I'm running sheep down the chute with Patricio — from Acapulco — who tells me how much he likes Wyoming. I say I'll take Acapulco any day, and he smiles. Ten winters he's been in Wyoming. A big ram shies, slips away and back through the funnel gate before it closes. Patricio, me, and a man I don't know run around flapping our arms trying to get that ram to go back toward the open gate. Sam, Johnny's favorite of the Border Collies, comes to help but gets awful excited, not used to moving sheep in a closed corral. Sam runs that big ram straight down the fence the wrong way. Instead of turning at the end, the ram slams head first into a steel gate, snaps its spine and collapses in the dust, foam oozing at its mouth, legs and feet twitching.

I bend down and feel along the neck. The ram's looking straight at me but not seeing a thing. I ask Johnny's son, "What're we gonna do?" He shrugs. I ask Patricio.

"Leave it."

We stand around for a while, the ram's tongue rolls out, spasms get stronger for about ten or fifteen minutes then stop. All three of us drag the dead sheep to the fence and hoist it over onto an unused patch of dust. Johnny tries lecturing Sam, but it's no use so the dog goes back to work. We do, too.

About three o'clock Jean Michel Labady comes around, makes small talk, jumps into a pen and wrestles with sheep for fun. Really he's making sure we don't shear a Labady sheep. John Miro shows up, too. Hangs around a while. About five we load their sheep in horse trailers and they take off.

The generator's shut down. People walk away wiping muddy sweat off their faces when somebody says, "What about that dead ram?" We go back, pick it up and kind of drag-haul it to the shearing trailer, shove it in. The fleece comes off, but slow. It's hard to manipulate a dead sheep — it's heavier, bent in peculiar positions, and can't turn when you shove.

The Australian shearer's cursing and cutting. It doesn't matter how much this one bleeds. Finally he stops, pushes the fleece out onto the platform and walks away to wash and eat and wait for tomorrow and more sheep. Johnny says it's ok to leave the ram's body there, we'll take care of it later.

Among People

Alone after working all day among people,
tired, I fall asleep on the couch, radio
playing softly. Voices come toward me —
"Attention!" and I sleepily turn the radio off.
But they continue, "Attention! You are directed
to leave this area. We are under nuclear attack.
Proceed south as quickly as possible. This
is not a test. We are under attack.
Please remain calm."

Half asleep, heart beating hard
so my throat feels the lump, I get up
and open the door — dusty air and red trails
of light percolating through it as a car
moves slowly up the road. No one in sight.

Groggy, I run to the horses,
saddle Trouble, put halters on the others,
ready to ride when I feel a fresh wind
on my face, clouds blowing away.
I look up at the stars and clear sky,
the silence and, awake, realize
someone is playing a joke.

I ride Trouble hard in the pasture,
let him run full speed toward a fence,
lean as he turns hard and gallops
the fence line. Around and around
the dark pasture until he slows on his own.
I get off and, eyes closed, without a brush,
rub him down with my hands — back and belly,
neck, mane, tail. I whisper in his ear,
press my lips to his face to taste the oils

in his hair. Dropping the saddle pad
on the ground and pulling Trouble's blanket
over my chest, I go to sleep in a field of horses,
the smell of their skin and sweat
rushing up my nose.

Fixing Fence

Pronghorn slows for a line of wire
then crosses under, a little fur
left on a barb, each steel star
a human eye. Running animal leans
into being. Crow caws,
hummingbird hovers and hums.

A thousand miles away two horses
hear the song from a cottonwood tree
and turn to look, but can't get closer.
Everything — the horses, a flower torn
from its stalk, a tumbleweed, brown
paper bag, blue piece of plastic,
snow driven in a wind, all of it —
piles up against the fence and stops.

The Horses Of The Poor

Among mules and goats they stand,
these gaunt ladies and gentlemen,

backs bowed, heads down.
With them I wait for blue skies

and green grass, clear water,
dry golden hay through the winter,

alfalfa sweet spring in which
to lie down and roll, scratching

our long backs, rubbing
our faces into the earth.

Winter Move

Dear Belem,

This is the day I hate,
the day we move the horses
from town to the ranch, from pasture
to thousands of acres of space
and light and cold, the only friends
prairie dog and sheep, the time
of year you walk up a draw
and likely as not you're gone for good.

There's no set day, but we know.
Sometimes it's the snow,
sometimes the wind and cold,
sometimes it's just a look in the sky,
a feeling you have about the air
and what's going to happen
for the next six months.

Is my real subject clear, Belem?
I don't know how to talk
when you're not here, your absent eyes
I look into, the nods of your head
and smiles, the almost inaudible mm-hmmm
you give me so I know we are conversing
and soon it is your turn. I realize
you won't ever get this note.
Even if you did, you could never answer.
I'm sorry how I started all this
and now we're apart, the years, burning.

Do you know what I do with these letters?
After they're sealed and addressed
I carry them out to the horses,

open the envelopes and, to those big
mute animals, read aloud. Then I burn
what I've read. I figure you'll hear it.

How can I give you winter?
If, where you are, there is a *lonchería*
or some other modern place, walk there
and ask for a cup of ice, hold this ice
in your bare hands, no matter how cold,
until it melts. Keep on holding the ice.

That's silly. You can put the ice
back in the cup. Oh, Belem, remember
the house in Soloita, the warm salty waves
at the beach and how we would go
every day after work to swim. Forgive me,
I'm sorry, shit, I already said that.

That first day of winter
the horses are hauled away
and released alone into a world
which, if harsher than any we can imagine,
is, at least, their own.

Clever Hans

To prove the intelligence of animals
Herr Von Osten taught his horse Hans mathematics.

Tapping out answers with his hoof, Hans
and his master toured Europe, amazing all

until it was observed that Hans could not answer
if he could not see his questioner,

and Herr Von Osten and the horse were denounced
as frauds. Clever Hans knew no mathematics.

He only calculated minute changes in human breathing,
the lift of an eyebrow, the flare of a nostril.

He can neither cipher nor read, they said,
and felt restored and relieved. How odd not to observe

that Hans answered our questions while we ignore
everything he asked us each and every day.

Feed

Never offered sugar
and unimpressed by the noise
he makes chewing carrots
and apples, Trouble likes
oats — long dry grains,
pale tan, the sides rolled
to the center like loaves
of Spanish bread. He stands
grinding away. Half the grain
falls to the ground
where later he'll scoop it up,
oats, horse spit and dust
making a muddy goo
of the feed. But Trouble
won't mind. He'll go ahead,
put it in his mouth and eat.

Harold's Idea

I scream horse and Margo's head
spins 360 degrees. But really
I didn't say horse at all. I said
"Whoa, whoa," as Harold gallops
toward the arena wall. I was learning
to ride English — feet out of the irons,
irons wrapped across the saddle —
when Harold got his idea.

I've often thought of this idea
that horses get, this private
communication urging them to run.

And I speculate about what
they are running from or toward —
snakes, a cloud, the barn, hay,
a voice, other horses, the sound
of a gun, truck or door, the caw
of a crow, a branch breaking
in the wind, a prairie dog's blink.

Could be anything — the invisible
sounds and smells and sights
in the mind of a horse.

No matter how hard I try to see
what Harold sees, or to stop
him from running, I can't,
and see only what Margo sees —
me falling, sliding off the right side
under the horse and into the dust
from which I rise and walk, stiffly,
in my two-legged human manner, away.

As Many Spirits As Stars

Dancing on cold across light
the ghosts of grasshoppers, horses and sheep,
the glittering crust I break with my boot
and step through a thousand years,
last summer's hard insect shell battering
my legs, my hands deep in the oily fleece,
the pale cloud from black nostrils.

Tonight's eyes that open, away from men.
I lean into a ravine, momentarily warm
to it all — this this. But Christ, it's
fifteen below and the wind is no woman
sweetly removing my clothes. Ripping
into my skin, she is the wind,
one of as many spirits as stars.

Wild Horse Race

It's not true that they're wild, just horses that haven't been halter broke, driven in by cowboys shouting and shooting and waving their arms. It makes the horses act crazy, look wilder. They're afraid, that fear terrible proof of the presence of an emotional life in horses.

At the rodeo the announcer's paid to make the day exciting so he says, "I want you good people to take a long look at the stored-up cussedness of these wild defiant vicious mustangs."

It's true the horses are battering the gates and arena fence, and most people in the audience have been kicked by a horse. Plunging hooves and rearing bodies crash against enclosures. Human shouting is mixed with every kind of horse scream. The handlers pulling on ropes tied to halters do seem to be containing what the announcer calls "pure brute animal force."

All day this goes on. An electric charge rises with the dust. Calf roping, bull riding, bronc busting, barrel racing, in the end the wild horse race. They'll be saddled and ridden and most likely some man will fall and be badly hurt — crushed leg or cracked head.

The afternoon becomes the smell of horse — shit and piss and fear, running and sweating and pulling until a rider ears his mount and everything stops. The dust settles and the day is transparent — boots, hats, saddles, halters, fences, all of it, you can see through like distilled water.

The rider takes the horse's ear in his mouth and bites. He hangs on, sinking his teeth in. Everything listens. There is no whip, spur or prod, only human teeth into horse's flesh, screams and dust, spit and blood, the taste of it, human face next to horse, their breathing, the rattle of phlegm in their throats, their flashing eyes. Each can smell the other's skin — the rancid oils they exude.

There are many bad jokes here about sex between animal and man. This much is true — the still flushed moment of the bite when horse and rider are one.

Raw

Dear Belem,

Today it's the wind reminds me
I'm raw, and easily flayed.
Another day it'll be the snow
or the insatiable heat
or a person who tells me I'm shit.

Last night the moon was at its highest point
in the sky for the year, and was full.
Harold, Trouble, P-Brain — all the horses —
laid back their ears, ready to kick.
Full moon always throws them off
and yesterday was the worst.

I don't think they know why —
like they're locked in the barn
and suddenly it's on fire.
They've got to bash down the doors,
sparks in their tails and manes,
hiss of hair, crackle of flame.

You know that feeling — trapped
and cornered and hot, a million moving
things buzzing around you, picking at you,
the world full up with stuff
while inside is emptiness,
infinite space no one can fill.

I suppose, Belem, it's unlikely
horses suffer this way, but they're scared.
Every month they whirl and snap.
Harold's got a fresh cut on his shoulder
the shape of the Bitch's teeth.
The Pony spent the morning standing alone

behind a mound of earth left when we dug
the pond. Trouble won't let P-Brain
stand beside him. They're all jumpy as hell.
Their skin glows as if the blood
shines right through the skin,
transparent and raw.

Awfully Warm For Late Fall

Today, facing each other back to back
and looking away, they lash out,
legs and feet meeting in air.

Neither sees the other,
ears flat along his head
and filled up with hate

because the wrong horse
came first to the old tire
full of oats and corn,

because a million years of standing
clannish at the tops of hills ready
at any moment to bolt cannot be erased

by some centuries of domestic bliss,
by tires full of oats and corn,
by winter hay and alfalfa cake,

cannot be erased — no matter
the season, no matter the temperature
on any given day.

Helping The Vet

"Mean stallions," Dr. Tom says,
"They're almost all mean, wound up
as tight as springs, waiting.
They've got to exercise hard,
wear themselves out." He's explaining
the hot walker to me — a conveyor belt
for horses to run on.

I'm tempted to say they might not be so mean
if they led a horse's life, but reluctant.
Tom knows a lot more than me. Besides,
I've seen wild stallions — mean sonsabitches.

Tom checks their feet and we move them,
close them in one behind the other,
walls pinching them from both sides,
mechanical floor beneath their feet,
no escape but upward,
and, though it's unlikely,
I wouldn't be surprised
to see these two fly,
rise out of this room
and take off through the sky
above Buffalo, two angry animal souls.
And secretly, whatever I've learned
of horses and men, I'd be gratified
to watch them go.

They run while Tom and I talk about medicine
for Trouble, who drove a piece of wire
two inches up his right front hoof. Somehow,
on the walker, the lead stallion turns
and bites the other, who rises on his hind legs

but, instead of flying, lifts fully up
and goes on over coming down on his back
and crushing his skull.

The lead horse is blood crazy now,
pawing and bashing the sidewalls.
Tom and I, we're stupid, standing there
until we run forward, get the live one
back in a stall and drag the dead horse
out to carry him away.

Glass Canyons

When President Reagan visited Baltimore,
police pushed a crowd of protesters
down the block and into the street
where, in Baltimore, it's illegal to stand.
Enforcing the law, policemen on horseback
charged the crowd, trampling one man.

How many horses in the high rise glass canyons,
galloping through the asphalt streets —
no sun burning through dry air,
no Bighorn Range rising from Buffalo
and dropping down to Ten Sleep,
no smell of sage and dust,
no greasewood, cottonwood or aspen.
Just Baltimore, and the policemen
on the backs of horses, driving
them forward into the crowd.

Winter Work Done, What Next?

I sit bundled in clothes to watch the light,
the air slipping away in a visible sigh.

I wait through fall, winter and spring to summer,
reaching out to grab me with its claws —

the wind's hot fingernails along my face,
the rain's fists hammering my body.

Unchallenged after one fight, the rain
retires, followed by erosion and dust.

We are not so much competitive as fierce —
each life spare and pushed to the edge —

cottonwoods along an empty creek, grasshoppers eating
the paint off cars, the bentonite soil gumbo or dust,

five acres to feed one sheep. But wait!
Before you give up and go, bend down and look closely —

there's new grass, and, more closely still,
the minute petals of a nameless blue flower.

From The Leiter Bar

I was telling BJ about this book of poems
I'm writing about the horses. Like me,
BJ's a poet so it's ok to talk poetry.
Unlike me, BJ's born and raised in Wyoming,
figures I get it all wrong, especially about
ranching, so I lean more literary, tell her
I'm gonna make a poem with all the horse cliches
I can think of like "Never look a gift horse
in the mouth" and "That's putting the cart
before the horse" or, you know, BJ, like
"You can lead a horse to water
but you can't make him drink" or her drink.

"Might be funny," BJ says, "Doesn't sound like much
of a poem, though," like she's mad, but BJ goes away
and a few days later shows up waving this
big brown Christmas envelope with holly
and bells around the edge and scribbling on it.
"Me and Bobby Moore went down to the Leiter Bar
and asked the crowd if anybody knew any old sayings
about horses. 'Well, if that ain't a horse
of a different color sort of a question'
somebody said. See, it worked," BJ told me.
Everybody sat around drinking beer and talking
about Christmas and horses and here they are —
"Horsin' around." "Get off your high horse."
"Wild horses couldn't stop me." "He's a hack."
"She's a filly." Later there were about
six people huddled there at the bar, snow
coming down harder, cliches turning toward sex:

Neighbor girl's not broke to saddle yet.
Old man Irruty's still hung like a horse.
Louis K. brags he was out riding bareback last night.
Somebody's a stud or thoroughbred and Louis

interrupts to say his ride was a real barrel racer.
Bobby drains his beer then says, "I gotta piss
like a racehorse" and steps outside into the snow.

I tell BJ I'm amazed. "There's more," she says —
"Trying to ride with your horse tied
to a post, you and whose horse,
hold your horses, chomping at the bit, a nag,
a workhorse, put him out to pasture, plain
as a horse, feeling your oats, straight
from the horse's mouth, acts like he's riding
a white horse, should be horsewhipped, trying
to sell a horse to a mule, can't pony up
to that man, uses her the way you wouldn't
use a horse, don't trust that man as far
as I can throw a horse, sucking on his bridle teeth."

Finally BJ comes up for air, smiling, says,
"There's one more — Adrien Justa
from the Trading Post in UCross said
he once knew a man almost as human as a horse."

The Fact Of The Matter

Dear Belem,

The fact of the matter is
we had everything, whether we could find a job
or not, whether we were rich or poor.

I didn't know it then, or had forgotten
so I stumbled through those days
as though a great crosswind had hit me unaware.

Now, Belem, here is the magic — today,
last week, last month, all this year, again
I have everything, and know it.

Desolation and space showed me,
the thinness of the air
and the absence of people,

a hailstorm battering the garden back into the earth
one August day, the sudden warmth of a January thaw
so that I cut wood in a t-shirt, and sweat.

The horses, too, show me. Both the music
that marks their passage when they run, hoofbeats
across the earth, what we call beautiful,

and those other things we deem ugly — the fly
walking on the horse's eye, the animal smells
befouling the air, the breech foal dead at birth,

all this teaching me to see, and to say what I see,
to tell you that however many worlds we cross,
they are all one world. As for another,

there is neither escape to, nor imprisonment within.
Fancy talk, Belem, muddying the message — I'm alive
and well and send you greetings
from an unknown province far away.

Unprepared

From South Carolina, John
visits in January. Crazy,
but he wants to feel it,
what he calls the "lunar
cold of Wyoming winter."

OK, John, let's go,
gotta put out feed.
But his gloves aren't good
and his pants aren't warm.
His jacket's for hiking
the boulevards, not for work.
Takes forever to saddle a horse.

We ride fifteen minutes
checking locations before
we get the truck.
When we stop John can't get
his feet out, boots
frozen to the stirrups.

I laugh at the warm-weather boy
as he pries himself free.
He understands winter
could hurt him. I see it
in his eyes, laugh to cover up.
We ride back and load the truck,
drive and dump bales of hay,
then warm up in the cabin.

Near sunset the sky
glows, the light enflames
the inert dull earth — lavender
and green on blue, long
shadowy knives turning

the brown grass to gold,
all the ordinary that
when we look, isn't.

Warm now, John suggests
a ride — "for fun."
"For fun?" I ask, "OK,
if you say so," and though
the temperature's dropped
and the world collapsed, we
get the bridles from the truck.
I warn John not to
put the cold metal
in the horse's mouth,
show him by putting the bridle
inside my coat under my arm
and waiting what seems a long time.

I take it out and touch
the bit with my tongue.
Immediate freeze and, stupidly,
I pull. The bit comes away
along with a dime size chunk
of flesh. Mouth full of blood,
I spit. The thick crimson
syrup drips onto snow and splatters.

John laughs now and stamps his feet,
forgetting the cold. "This is
good," he says. "Just who
is the tourist?" And I admit
he's got a point as I too laugh
and spit more blood, thinking
before John leaves for South Carolina
I'll have to give him
my good warm boots.

Birds Too Fat To Fly

John tells Margo she is placid.
She worries he secretly means bland.
But one bright fall day she saw
a group of eagles — Golden and Bald —
feeding on a carcass. They
were like vultures, so full
they couldn't leave the ground.
They lurched up and down
the hillside relearning the lessons
of their youth. They were,
Margo told me, "Birds too fat to fly."
And laughed, "What a great phrase —
think of Trouble, Harold and Penelope
alone together on winter range
and when we go to get them,
we have to coax them in, shake
cans of oats and promise them endless
warm barns and clear fresh water
and no saddles." Then she makes up
their phrase — "They're horses
too quick to catch." It's a game.
I say the sky is the sky
too blue to believe. "Come on,"
Margo sweetly taunts, "You can
do better than that." And throws me,

 Cold too bitter to breathe.

 Draws too deep to defend.

 Erosion too aged to erase.

 Grass too gone to green.

She really laughs at that last
and names the whole: "Ranching
too disastrous to deny."
But who cares —
happiness too holy to humble
and life too lovely to lose.
She puts her arms around me
and stands placidly motionless,
whispers in my ear, "Birds
too fat to fly . . . "

Moving Cows, Steve's

Looks easy this time — no trailers, no trucks, no loony long drive. All we have to do is saddle Trouble and Penelope, ride three miles out the old road along the Interstate, cross at the underpass into Steve's pasture and move his cows a mile or so into another pasture. Easy.

Steve's a CPA, which means he's got enough money to lease some land, but not enough time to work it. The trick about moving these cows is that the two pastures aren't exactly adjacent. One juts down into the other in the shape of an L with the gate at the corner. If the cows don't want to go through the gate, they can turn right and follow the fence line away, or they can take a step to the left and run straight up the vertical of the L, farther and farther from the gate and picking up speed all the time.

Margo's on Trouble and I'm riding Penelope. I'm calling her Penelope, hoping that if she doesn't hear the name P-Brain she won't screw up. Everything goes fine at first. We cross the ditches with almost no stumbling, trot easily through the cottonwoods along the creek around downed branches and across holes. Both horses calmly ford the stream and we bring the cows back in a bunch. They amble sweetly toward the new pasture until one of them notices the open gate and shakes her head at the idea. Her idea infects the others and they splay out in three directions.

Margo gallops far off to my right and pushes the cows back toward me. Penelope and I run in a line before them trying to make them turn. Miraculously they do, and stream through the gate, true as water cut into a field. About half through, an older cow leans to the left and runs hard up the L. I go after her, cutting wide to turn her back when she decides to veer away from the fence line. But she doesn't veer, instead making a right angle turn away. Ms. P and I lean into it but our sharp turn isn't sharp enough and horse, rider and cow slide around each other in a careening figure eight.

I know we'll get the cow back eventually, but I'm thinking of Steve and how he said to take it easy. "Remember," he reminded me, "Every time a cow runs, she loses weight, and every pound off's a lost dollar."

So the longer I take to get this cow through the gate, the less money she brings in and the less I'm worth, watching the dollar signs click downward. I make one more looping circle and Ms. P convinces the cow to turn twice and stay in line toward the gate till she's through it with the others and that's that, but I don't know if Steve's going to like the price, him being a CPA, and the cows being commodities getting thinner all the time.

May I Present

Dear Belem,

I am as deeply in love
as I could be, and you are dead.
There, I've said it aloud
for the first time — dead.

Are you smiling at me, Belem?
Looking down on my childish refusals
from some place above Powder River Pass,
above the Cloud Peaks, from the clarity
of that world into the murkiness
of this one? Both are empty — Wyoming
and Heaven — with neither cities nor trees
to block the view. I won't speak for there,
but the still solemnity of Wyoming
deepens the distance of sight.

Belem, this is Margo. She is the one
I love as much as you. And these
are the horses —Trouble, with the white stripe
on his nose; Penelope, whose hair is coppery;
and Harold, the beat-up bay.

You'll like them, Belem,
and they'll be happy that, finally,
I present them to you.

Our Lady

At home or in town
Margo's motto is
"Close enough" and
"Oh well."

But here, fifty miles from
a post office, gas station
or grocery, she is
another Margo,

Our Lady of Exactitude,
whose step is
like the sky —
thoughtless, and perfect.

Outside Wyoming

There is a world and it is full.
Here we are measured
by what is absent, the rain
that is reluctant to fall.

The joke is there are more pronghorn
than people. It's true, and
there are more sheep than pronghorn,
more grasshoppers than sheep.

When the cold descends it's a lid
hammered shut. The heat flattens
the summer grass and everything burns
to gold but the animals we have to sell.

"What a place," you say, "Who would
want to live there?" The answer
is another truth not so much
hard to explain as unused to being said.

Putting Out Feed

Winter dry and cold enough my fingers bleed,
a little red seeping through my wool gloves,
I was feeding sheep, in this season
as odd and fragile as baby birds.

Worn down by winter's toll,
I grabbed an old ram
and jammed my hands into its fleece,
heavy with oil, and warm.

Wyoming, In Memoriam

No one is coming toward you,
and many are battering at the gate
to leave. Winter is long then one day
it is summer, choking on heat.

The ranches are lost,
the mines have closed,
the tourists have other
more appealing places to go.

Alone tonight, we sleep
within the silence of stars.
Coyote and mountain lion walk the ridge lines.
Pronghorn slip under the fences still standing.

But even as people leave, strange newcomers appear
in pick-ups marked Texaco and Mobil and Exxon.
Though they will not stay, they stop — breathless —
and stare sideways at the nearby sky.

They scrape away the sad cactus, frozen
and stunted, the twisted solitary tree,
the thin yellow grass, until the earth is bare,
and they drill, 6000 feet and more.

Those of us who watch
learn there is nothing we can do.
As we ignored the exodus,
so we try to ignore this entry,

to continue walking
from place to place,
in memoriam,
to saddle a horse and ride.

Search

1.

Deep in winter,
between Wormwood and Four Mile,
I find myself stalking horses.
Putting my ear to the ground,
I let my heartbeat slow
to that of the planet
and my breathing stops.

2.

I carry no tools —
no knives, no guns,
no special whistles
beyond the range of human hearing,
no high-powered binoculars.
I wrap a bag of oats in a halter
and sling it over my shoulder
like a bedroll, like a compass,
and I begin to walk.
Halfway up each draw
and perpendicular to the cut
I begin looking both directions
deep into shadow.
Twenty thousand acres like this
I cross and there is nothing —
an eagle's nest
without a bird,
a leafless cottonwood tree,
the frozen ground
devoid of snow,
the raw blue sky

absent clouds.
At every hoof print I pause,
inspect it — the freshly turned earth
or worn impression.
Sometimes I stop,
squat on my heels and wait.

3.

Hours pass. The shadows
grow longer but stay fastened
to the hills. I walk in circles,
crossing and recrossing the same draws.
Several days gone by I turn
and climb a ridge line
to scan the horizon
for the still silhouette of horse,
then I turn again
and climb down, touching the ground,
seeking traces, something
I could bend over and pick up,
something redolent of horse.

4.

Finally at dusk
I see them, or
think I do, then
realize I've seen myself,
four-footed and sure,
far out ahead of another horse,
running through a narrow channel,
my nostrils open wide,

the frozen air biting
into soft blackness.
Some sound comes calling me
then answering me, cooing,
screaming and I turn, dizzyingly,
turn and turn and turn
until I fall.

5.

When I rise it is dark
and I am dreamless.
There is a sticky warm spot
behind my right ear.
I rub my hand across it
and come away with blood.
I taste it,
wipe my hand on my pants,
wrap my handkerchief over the lump
and again walk,
this time checking my footprints,
curious whose track it is I leave.

Before Wyoming

Dear Belem,

In the Bible it is said
before the world was the void
and it was formless and vast
until all, under the hand of God,
rose from it. Light was made separate
from dark, the earth from the firmament,
shore from sea. All was distinguished
and defined. Before Wyoming

there was you, and Mexico.
Before that I was elsewhere and alive,
a child in the Langell Valley
and at Cape Hurricane, on the coast.
Later I stared across the Sonora Desert
at the Santa Catalina Mountains.
It is surprising I was so close to you
even then. I ate meals and slept in beds.
There was school and home.
I fell in love again and again.

As a young man I stood on the border
of two hostile states. Strangers
shot at me. I heard languages
I could not speak. The world's grace
was as great as its sorrow.

All these details, Belem — the names
and times and roads and rooms,
the circuitous way I came to this place
where biography and landscape rush to be one.

Supermarket Horse

In Denver, in the grocery,
we found the horse, blood red,
fading chipped paint, eyes wide
and legs bent forever in gallop.

"Old horse," I said aloud,
"Like from a dream carousel."
And remembered my mother
putting a dime in the slot
long ago. I looked and saw
this horse took a penny,
just one cent — impossible
ancient horse. Where are the lines,
the children calling out,
the adults happy to please?

The horse was alone,
so we climbed onto its back,
both of us, and the children
stared, and their parents,
the checkers and bag boys,
the floor manager and uniformed cop,
they all stared as we
put in our penny and rode.